A

World Art Series
VAN GOGH
by Parker Tyler/92 color plates

Doubleday & Company, Inc.   Garden City, New York   1968

Library of Congress Catalog Card Number: 68-23387
All rights reserved
This book is fully protected by copyright under
the terms of the International Copyright Union
Permission to use portions of this book must be
obtained in writing from the publisher
First published in Japan
English-language edition first published
in Japan in September 1968
Printed in Japan

Van Gogh

1 — *Self-portrait before His Easel*   1888/Oil/65.5 x 50.5cm/Stedelijk Museum, Amsterdam
2 — *The Mender*   1881/Pencil and Water Color/62.5 x 47.5cm/Rijksmuseum Kröller-Müller, Otterlo
3 — *Crouching Youth with Sickle*   1881/Pencil and Water Color/47.0 x 61.0cm/Rijksmuseum Kröller-Müller, Otterlo
4 — *Woods at The Hague with Young Girl in White*   1882/Oil/39.0 x 59.0cm/Rijksmuseum Kröller-Müller, Otterlo
5 — *Fisherman by the Sea*   1883/Oil/50.0 x 32.0cm/Rijksmuseum Kröller-Müller, Otterlo
6 — *The Basket Maker*   1884/Oil/Private Collection, Paris
7 — *Leaving the Church at Nuenen*   1884/Oil/42.0 x 33.0cm/Stedelijk Museum, Amsterdam
8 — *Head of a Peasant with Pipe*   1884/Oil/44.0 x 32.0cm/Rijksmuseum Kröller-Müller, Otterlo
9 — *Portrait of a Young Woman*   1885/Oil/152.5 x 127.0cm/Pushkin Museum, Moscow
10 — *Bullock Attached to a Cart*   1884/Oil/57.0 x 82.5cm/Rijksmuseum Kröller-Müller, Otterlo
11 — *Cottage at the Day's End*   1885/Oil/65.5 x 79.5cm/Stedelijk Museum, Amsterdam
12 — *The Potato-Eaters*   1885/Oil/81.5 x 114.5cm/Stedelijk Museum, Amsterdam
13 — *The Potato-Eaters*   1885/Oil/72.0 x 93.0cm/Rijksmuseum Kröller-Müller, Otterlo
14 — *Torso of a Woman*   1886/Oil/73.0 x 54.0cm/Private Collection, Zurich
15 — *Self-portrait*   1886/Oil/47.0 x 35.0cm/Private Collection, Paris
16 — *Lady beside a Cradle*   1887/Oil/61.0 x 46.0cm/Stedelijk Museum, Amsterdam
17 — *Père Tanguy*   1887/Oil/92.0 x 73.0cm/Musée Rodim, Paris
18 — *View of Paris from Vincent's Room in the rue Lepic*   1887/Oil/46.5 x 38.5cm/Stedelijk Museum, Amsterdam
19 — *The Yellow Books*   1887/Oil/73.0 x 93.0cm/Private Collection, Swiss
20 — *Flowers in Blue Vase*   1887/Oil/61.0 x 38.0cm/Rijksmuseum Kröller-Müller, Otterlo
21 — *Self-portrait (detail)*   1887/Oil/32.0 x 23.0cm/Rijksmuseum Kröller-Müller, Otterlo
22 — *The Bridge at Chatou*   1887/Oil/52.0 x 65.0cm/Private Collection, Zurich
23 — *Lark over Wheatfield*   1887/Oil/54.5 x 65.5cm/Stedelijk Museum, Amsterdam
24 — *Caravans at a Gypsy Camp*   1888/Oil/45.0 x 51.0cm/The Louvre, Paris
25 — *Truck-gardens*   1888/Oil/73.0 x 92.0cm/Stedelijk Museum, Amsterdam
26 — *Orchard in Bloom, Bordered by Cypresses*   1888/Oil/65.0 x 81.0cm/Rijksmuseum Kröller-Müller, Otterlo
27 — *Trees in Bloom, Souvenir of Mauve*   1888/Oil/73.0 x 59.5cm/Rijksmuseum Kröller-Müller, Otterlo
28 — *Bridge at Arles, Pont de Langlois*   1888/Oil/54.0 x 65.0cm/Rijksmuseum Kröller-Müller, Otterlo
29 — *Bridge at Arles, Pont de Langlois (detail)*
30 — *The Yellow House: Vincent's House at Arles*   1888/Oil/72.0 x 92.0cm/Stedelijk Museum, Amsterdam
31 — *Café Terrace, Evening*   1888/Oil/81.0 x 65.5cm/Rijksmuseum Kröller-Müller, Otterlo
32 — *Haystacks in Provence*   1888/Oil/73.0 x 92.5cm/Rijksmuseum Kröller-Müller, Otterlo
33 — *Starry Night on the Rhône*   1888/Oil/72.5 x 92.0cm/Private Collection, Paris
34 — *Portrait of a Man*   1889-90/Oil/65.0 x 54.5cm/Rijksmuseum Kröller-Müller, Otterlo
35 — *Young Man with a Cap*   1888/Oil/47.5 x 39.0cm/Private Collection, Zurich
36 — *The Sower*   1888/Oil/64.0 x 80.0cm/Rijksmuseum Kröller-Müller, Otterlo
37 — *The Sower (detail)*
38 — *View of Arles with Flowering Trees*   1888/Oil/54.0 x 65.5cm/Stedelijk Museum, Amsterdam
39 — *La Berceuse*   1889/Oil/92.0 x 73.0cm/Rijksmuseum Kröller-Müller, Otterlo

40 — *Gauguin's Armchair*   1888/Oil/91.0 x 73.0cm/Stedelijk Museum, Amsterdam
41 — *Sunflowers*   1888/Oil/76.0 x 59.0cm/Private Collection
42 — *Park with People: The Poet's Garden*   1888/Oil/73.0 x 92.0cm/Rijksmuseum Kröller-Müller, Otterlo
43 — *Pollard Willows (detail)*   1888/Oil/31.5 x 34.5cm/Rijksmuseum Kröller-Müller, Otterlo
44 — *The Sower*   1888/Oil/33.0 x 40.5cm/Stedelijk Museum, Amsterdam
45 — *Self-portrait*   1888/Oil/Private Collection, Zurich
46 — *Bedroom of Vincent van Gogh at Arles*   1889/Oil/73.0 x 92.0cm/Stedelijk Museum, Amsterdam
47 — *Still Life: Iris*   1889/Oil/92.5 x 74.0cm/Stedelijk Museum, Amsterdam
48 — *Still Life with Onions*   1889/Oil/50.0 x 64.0cm/Rijksmuseum Kröller-Müller, Otterlo
49 — *The Alps: Mountain Country near Saint-Rémy*   1890/Oil/59.0 x 72.0cm/Rijksmuseum Kröller-Müller, Otterlo
50 — *Peach-tree in Bloom*   1888/Oil/65.5 x 81.5cm/Courtauld Institute of Art, London
51 — *Hospital Garden at the Convent of St. Paul*   1889/Oil/95.0 x 75.0cm/Rijksmuseum Kröller-Müller, Otterlo
52 — *Cypresses with Figures of Two Women*   1889/Oil/92.0 x 73.0cm/Rijksmuseum Kröller-Müller, Otterlo
53 — *Mower in Wheatfield*   1889/Oil/73.5 x 93.0cm/Stedelijk Museum, Amsterdam
54 — *Mower in Wheatfield (detail)*
55 — *Peasant Woman Binding Wheat (after Millet)*   1889/Oil/44.0 x 33.5cm/Stedelijk Museum, Amsterdam
56 — *The Evening Walk*   1889/Oil/49.0 x 45.0cm/Museum and Art Gallery, São-Paulo
57 — *Grove of Olive Trees*   1889/Oil/72.0 x 92.0cm/Rijksmuseum Kröller-Müller, Otterlo
58 — *Olive-gathering*   1889/Oil/73.0 x 92.0cm/Rijksmuseum Kröller-Müller, Otterlo
59 — *Ravine in the Peyroulets*   1889/Oil/72.0 x 92.0cm/Rijksmuseum Kröller-Müller, Otterlo
60 — *Wheatfield with Tree in the Mountains*   1889/Oil/73.0 x 91.5cm/Rijksmuseum Kröller-Müller, Otterlo
61 — *The Resurrection of Lazarus (after Rembrandt)*   1889/Oil/48.5 x 63.0cm/Stedelijk Museum, Amsterdam
62 — *The Good Samaritan (after Delacroix)*   1890/Oil/73.0 x 60.0cm/Rijksmuseum Kröller-Müller, Otterlo
63 — *Haystack after a Rainy Day*   1889/Oil/64.0 x 52.5cm/Rijksmuseum Kröller-Müller, Otterlo
64 — *Road with Cypress and Star (detail)*   1890/Oil/92.0 x 73.0cm/Rijksmuseum Kröller-Müller, Otterlo
65 — *Dr. Gachet's Garden*   1890/Oil/73.0 x 52.0cm/The Louvre, Paris
66 — *Grieving Man*   1890/Oil/81.0 x 65.0cm/Rijksmuseum Kröller-Müller, Otterlo
67 — *Field of Poppies*   1890/Oil/71.0 x 91.0cm/Kunsthalle, Bremen
68 — *Study of Cows*   1890/Oil/55.0 x 65.0cm/Musée des Beaux-Arts, Lille
69 — *Street in Auvers*   1890/Oil/73.0 x 92.0cm/National Museum, Helsinki
70 — *Landscape with Three Trees and a Cottage*   1890/Oil/64.0 x 78.0cm/Rijksmuseum Kröller-Müller, Otterlo
71 — *Cottages at Cordeville*   1890/Oil/73.0 x 92.0cm/The Louvre, Paris
72 — *The Church at Auvers*   1890/Oil/73.0 x 92.0cm/The Louvre, Paris
73 — *The House at Auvers*   1890/Oil/50.5 x 101.0cm/Stedelijk Museum, Amsterdam
74 — *Staircase at Auvers*   1890/Oil/49.8 x 70.0cm/City Art Museum, St. Louis
75 — *Wheatfield with Crows*   1890/Oil/51.0 x 103.5cm/Stedelijk Museum, Amsterdam
76 — *Portrait of Dr. Gachet*   1890/Oil/66.0 x 57.0cm/The Louvre, Paris
77 — *Mlle. Gachet in the Garden*   1890/Oil/46.0 x 55.5cm/The Louvre, Paris
78 — *Wheatfield under a Stormy (Blue) Sky (detail)*   1890/Oil/50.5 x 101.5cm/Stedelijk Museum, Amsterdam

DESSINS

The Sower (after Millet)
Woman Sewing
Boulevard de Clichy
On the Paris Fortification
In the Suburbs of Paris
Harvest on the Plain of Crau
Vincent Van Gogh's Home at Arles
The Garden Behind the House
Young Girl With Shawl
The Farm of Père Eloi at Auvers
Willow Grove and Shepherd
View from the Hospital

VAN GOGH

1
elf-portrait before
His Easel
1888   65.5 x 50.5cm

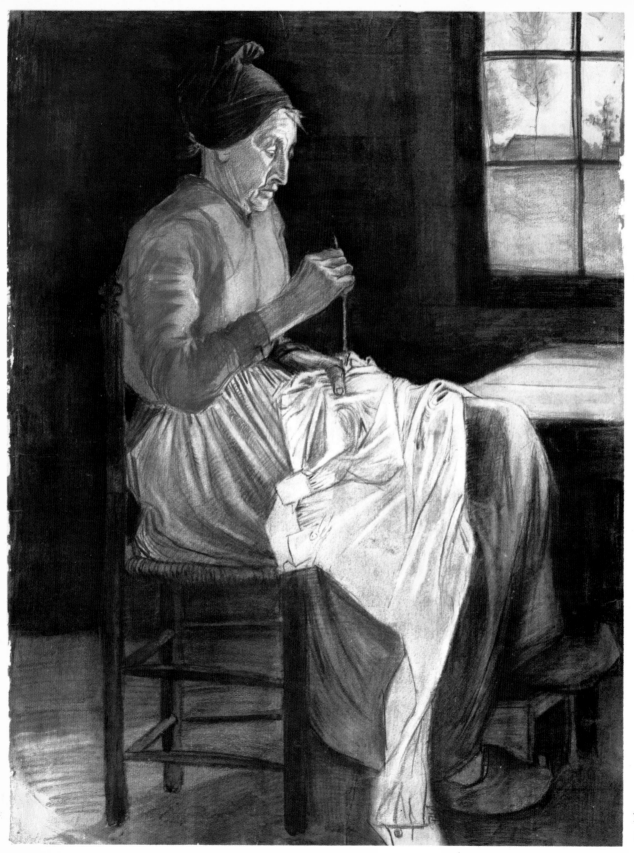

2 *The Mender*

1881   62.5 x 47.5cm

3   *Crouching Youth with Sickle*   1881   47.0 x 61.0cm

4 *Woods at The Hague with Young Girl in White*   1882   39.0 x 59.0cm

5 *Fisherman by the Sea*
   1883   50.0 x 32.0cm

6   *The Basket Maker*   1884

7   *Leaving the Church at Nuenen*   1884   42.0 x 33.0cm

8　*Head of a Peasant with Pipe*　1884　44.0 x 32.0cm

9   *Portrait of a Young Woman*   1885   152.5 x 127.0cm

10   *Bullock Attached to a Cart*   1884   57.0 x 82.5cm

11   *Cottage at the Day's End*   1885   65.5 x 79.5cm

12 *The Potato-Eaters* 1885 81.5 x 114.5cm

13 *The Potato-Eaters* 1885   72.0 x 93.0cm

14   *Torso of a Woman*   1886   73.0 x 54.0cm

15 *Self-portrait* 1886 47.0 x 35.0cm

16 *Lady beside a Cradle* 1887 61.0 x 46.0cm

17 *Père Tanguy* 1887 92.0 x 73.0cm

← 18   *View of Paris from Vincent's Room in the rue Lepic*   1887   46.5 x 38.5cm
19   *The Yellow Books*   1887   73.0 x 93.0cm

20 *Flowers in Blue Vase* 1887 61.0 x 38.0c

21 *Self-portrait* 1887 32.0 x 23.0cm →

22 *The Bridge at Chatou* 1887 52.0 x 65.0cm

23 *Lark over Wheatfield* 1887   54.5 x 65.5cm

24 *Caravans at a Gypsy Camp* 1888   45.0 x 51.0cm

25 *Truck-gardens* 1888 73.0 x 92.0cm

26   *Orchard in Bloom, Bordered by Cypresses*   1888   65.0 x 81.0cm

27   *Trees in Bloom, Souvenir of Mauve*   1888   73.0 x 59.5cm →

Souvenir de Mauve
Vincent

28/29   *Bridge at Arles, Pont de Langlois*   1888   54.0 x 65.0cm

30 *The Yellow House: Vincent's House at Arles*   1888   72.0 x 92.0cm
31 *Café Terrace, Evening*   1888   81.0 x 65.5cm →

32 *Haystacks in Provence*   1888   73.0 x 92.5cm

33 *Starry Night on the Rhône* 1888 72.5 x 92.0cm

34 *Portrait of a Man* 1889-90 65.0 x 54.5cm

35   *Young Man with a Cap*   1888   47.5 x 39.0cm

36/37 *The Sower* 1888   64.0 x 80.5cm

38 *View of Arles with Flowering Trees*   1888   54.0 x 65.5cm
39 *La Berceuse*   1889   92.0 x 73.0cm →

40 *Gauguin's Armchair*   1888   91.0 x 73.0cm

41 *Sunflowers* 1888 76.0 x 59.0cm

42 *Park with People: The Poet's Garden*   1888   73.0 x 92.0cm

43 *Pollard Willows* 1888 31.5 x 34.5cm

44 *The Sower* 1888 33.0 x 40.5cm

← 45 *Self-portrait*   1888
46 *Bedroom of Vincent van Gogh at Arles*   1889   73.0 x 92.0cm

← 47 *Still Life: Iris* 1889 92.5 x 74.0cm
48 *Still Life with Onions* 1889 50.0 x 64.0cm

49 *The Alps: Mountain Country near Saint-Rémy* 1890 59.0 x 72.0cm

50 *Peach-tree in Bloom* 1888 65.5 x 81.5cm

51 *Hospital Garden at the Convent of St. Paul*   1889   95.0 x 75.0cm

52 *Cypresses with Figures of Two Women* 1889 92.0 x 73.0cm

53/54   *Mower in Wheatfield*   1889   73.5 x 93.0cm

55   *Peasant Woman Binding Wheat (after Millet)*   1889   44.0 x 33.5cm

56   *The Evening Walk*   1889   49.0 x 45.0cm

57   *Grove of Olive Trees*   1889   72.0 x 92.0cm

58   *Olive-gathering*   1889   73.0 x 92.0cm

59 *Ravine in the Peyroulets* 1889 72.0 x 92.0cm

60 *Wheatfield with Tree in the Mountains* 1889 73.0 x 91.5cm

61   *The Resurrection of Lazarus (after Rembrandt)*   1889   48.5 x 63.0cm
62   *The Good Samaritan (after Delacroix)*   1890   73.0 x 60.0cm →

63   *Haystack after a Rainy Day*   1889   64.0 x 52.5cm
64   *Road with Cypress and Star*   1890   92.0 x 73.0cm →

65 *Dr. Gachet's Garden*
1890 73.0 x 52.0cm

66 *Grieving Man* 1890 81.0 x 65.0cm

67 *Field of Poppi*
1890 71.0 x 91.0cm

68   *Study of Cows*   1890   55.0 x 65.0cm

69 *Street in Auvers* 1890 73.0 x 92.0cm

70 *Landscape with Three Trees and a Cottage* 1890 64.0 x 78.0cm

71   *Cottages at Cordeville*   1890   73.0 x 92.0cm
72   *The Church at Auvers*   1890   92.5 x 75.0cm →

73   *The House at Auvers*   1890   50.5 x 101.0cm

74 *Staircase at Auvers* 1890 49.8 x 70.0cm

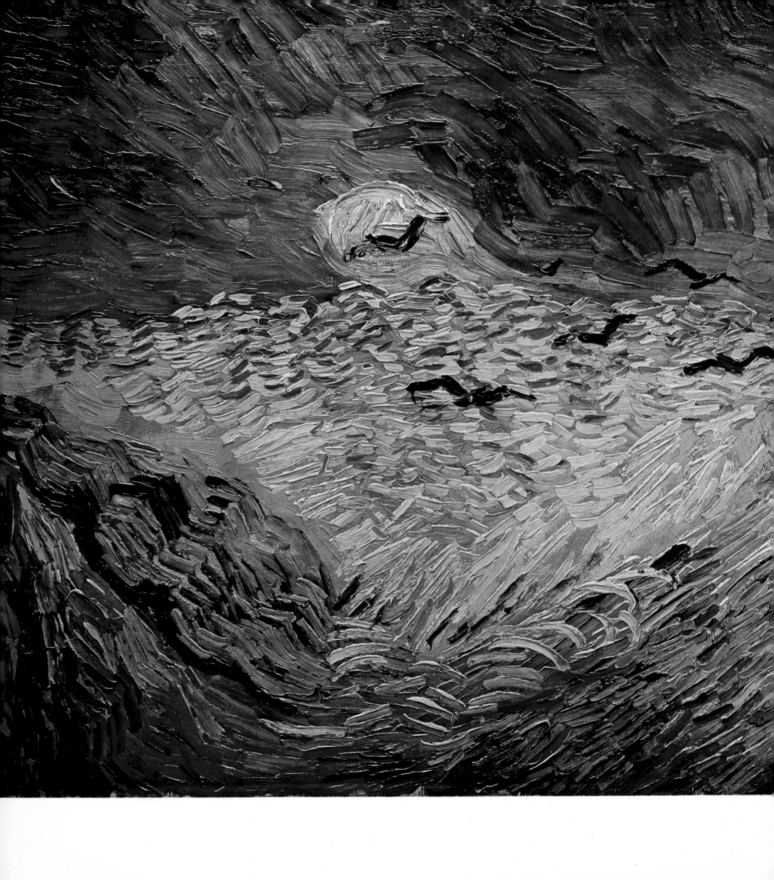

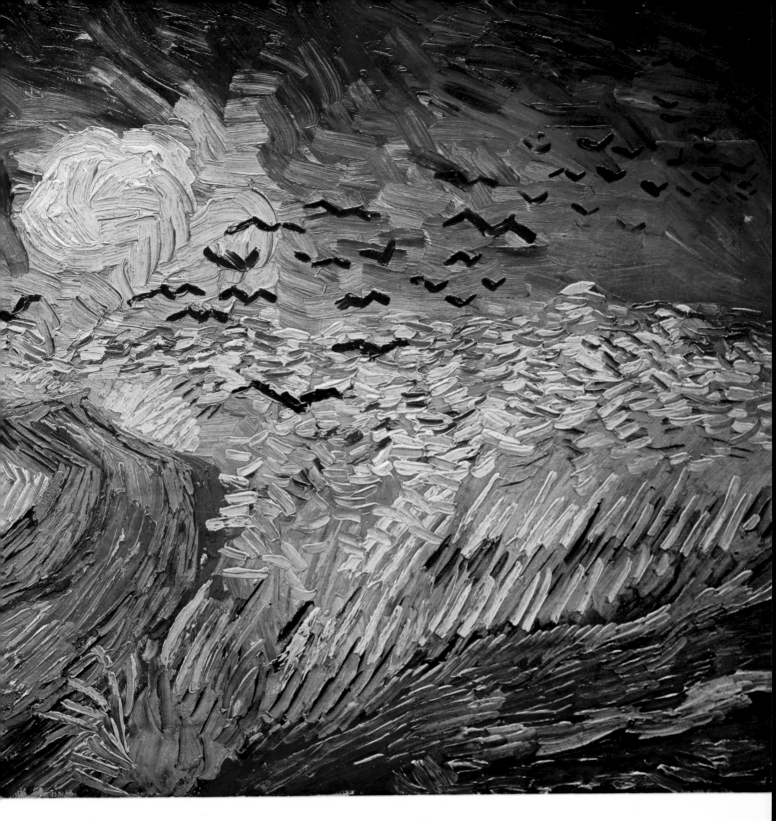

75   *Wheatfield with Crows*   1890   51.0 x 103.5cm

←76　*Portrait of Dr. Gachet*　1890　66.0 x 57.0cm

77　*Mlle. Gachet in the Garden*　1890　46.0 x 55.5cm

VAN GOGH

The life of Vincent van Gogh, born in 1853 the son and grandson of Dutch Protestant ministers, was a series of dramatic, sometimes violent internal and external reactions — a drastic kind of interpolar friction that persecuted him all his life. Possibly in the case of no other painter, even of modern times, can we find so unstable and difficult a temperament together with a legacy of works produced steadily, sometimes bountifully, from the year he decided to become a painter, 1880, till his death by suicide ten years later. Vincent van Gogh had lost the battle of himself when he was only 37. But by long odds he had won the battle of art. It makes a paradoxical and intriguing history, this phenomenal career, one that is still a challenge, in fact, to critics and biographers. It has been, in one sense, too easy to grasp the "drama" of van Gogh's life, its tragedy, its personal anguish and its deplorable issue (about a year before he died) of confinement in an insane asylum; yes, much too easy—because, while we can sympathize with the private frustration of a self-evident genius, we may well be as baffled as van Gogh himself when trying to identify the causes and composition of his life-problem.

Passing admiringly from one work to another, thrilled at the blaze of color, the release of sheer energy in terms of plastic form, one may wonder what could be thought of these pictures, in human terms, if they were the products of an unknown artist, or of someone whose private life (for some reason) had no records. Of course, the life of the artist who signed his canvases only with his given name (when he did sign them) has ample documentation, including a long series of virtually confessional letters to his younger brother, Theo. We learn a great deal about his inner struggles, which according to his explicit testimony revolved about his love for people, for humanity, and his unsolved dilemma in finding proper expression for this love. By no means did he first choose painting as a medium. Painting, in fact, may be called his "last resort" as a means of personal expression: the love he always talked about and whose nature he could never precisely define, but which lived in him like a hunger for some unknown food. At last this "food" became simply his vision of the world.

Vincent van Gogh's career has a way of provoking very modern questions about life as a moral project. What is the importance of psychology and of sex in studying the roots of his personal anguish, which was always preoccupied with "love"? Some might think that we ought not to probe too far into the private man who was van Gogh, that he suffered enough

Van Gogh as a young man

from lack of self-realization when young—or rather, from the abortive desire *for* self-realization—and that his failure, which had such tragic consequences, is one of those facts so stark, so irrevocable, that it makes superfluous our technical inquiries into cause and condition. Yet this is an attitude, I think, which van Gogh would have disapproved and found unreasonable. Always he himself *probed.* When he dwelt in the glorious light of Provence and transported its sights to canvas, he did not cease to have his problems; in fact, it was after his best, most productive year in painting, 1888—when he thought he had found a sort of Paradise in Arles—that his worst breakdown came: a series of attacks that led to physical violence and internment in the asylum at Saint-Rémy.

As a student and admirer of van Gogh's works, one cannot quite be at rest without inquiring into the enigma of his private self, whose deep disquiet he literally communicated to the works of his mature style. Though respectful of family tradition, he did not originally think himself destined for the ministry. His first gesture toward an occupation came when he obtained a job at an art gallery in The Hague, just sold to Goupil of Paris by one of his two uncles who both owned art galleries. Only sixteen, the young man was not quite neat in appearance and not altogether tactful in handling customers. He was transferred first to Goupil's Brussels branch and then to London. Doubtless he was too unhappy to sense his own vocation although he was right next to it. In London, to climax the awkwardness of his position, he promptly falls in love with his landlady's daughter and proposes marriage; rejected, he categorically rates himself a total personal failure, leaves London, goes to Paris for a while, and then, as if perversely, back to London. This exaggerated sensitivity and vacillation are supposed to be rather common to groping, emotional youth. But all of six years have gone by and Vincent decides to have another try with Goupil in Paris.

His employers had found him too aggressive; that is, he was not an ideal salesman. This was not because he was unsympathetic to art or unknowledgeable of it; on the contrary, now in Paris, he frequents the Louvre and is especially attracted to Millet. When Goupil again dismisses him from its employ, it is simply because he cannot get along with people. The general trouble is not hard to unriddle: he wanted all the intimacies and reassurance of personal congeniality (including love) and found them denied him. The curious thing about this biographic evidence is that we

A letter by Van Gogh

Sorrow, 1882

have no certainty as to just what Vincent offered people in the way of affection and what he expected in return. Whatever sexual contacts he had at this period evidently did not make him happy or satisfied.

The temptation is great to conceive Vincent van Gogh as a psychopathic case, where psychoanalysis might be very serviceable. But we have too little concrete internal evidence to yield to this temptation; rightly, we can deal only in terms of suggestion and speculation. Surely Vincent's sexuality was oddly dislocated and perhaps, unconsciously, he was physically attracted to men in a way which automatically became taboo and tacitly inspired horror in him. I say "perhaps" because van Gogh the man must remain predominantly an enigma. However, by dealing directly with what is self-evident and with things we can learn of him, we may speculate with some confidence. Assuming in Vincent a kind of retarded, amorphous sexuality, undetermined as to specific object, we can account for the aggressiveness he displayed toward men, an aggressiveness which meant resentment that they did not respond to his innocently affectionate overtures. On the other hand, the clumsy ways which would make it hard for him, later on, even to collect the boarding fees of religious students when he began teaching under a minister, may have arisen from the hostility that erotically underconfident men have for all males as sexual rivals. In any case, Vincent found himself regularly "oversusceptible." Regardless of circumstance, he reacted too personally, too directly, to both men and women.

In Paris, he was giving himself much to reading and brooding over human passions and human wrongs in the novels of Tolstoy and Dostoevsky. Losing his job at Goupil's struck him as partly the bitterness of the great human burden of being luckless and misunderstood. Speaking French properly was itself a hardship for this eager Dutchman with a morbidly sensitive amour-propre. Perhaps he could *still* save himself by saving others and so he turned again to the message of the Bible and its symbolic power as consolation. Yet he had to prove himself gradually. Then, returning to London, he obtained successive posts under two Protestant ministers and became "something," as he said, "between a minister and a missionary." However, when he wished to bring the Gospels to the miners because his desire was "to comfort the humble," he again met anticlimax. It seemed he was "too young."

Returning to Holland to spend Christmas with his parents in 1876, he tried bookselling without success and then decided that perhaps he needed more training to serve God as an evangelist but lacked the self-confidence to enter the Theological Seminary in Amsterdam. Always there is in Vincent the idea to distract his attention from himself and give it to others: this is a driving, insatiable impulse. If he cannot succeed in giving himself personally, he will do so collectively. It was not the joyous parts of the Bible that attracted him but the gloomiest, the most terrible, for we find in his surviving Bible that it is such passages he marked. This explains his preference for doing what he finally managed to do: go among the most forlorn and miserable of mining communities to bring the Gospels. In radical Protestant style, his desire is to be an individual savior, to make himself Christ's viceroy with the sacred books in his hand. Success now will solve the problem of all wounded self-suspicion, all self-depreciation.

Montmartre, 1886

Traditionally, sin and ignorance go together as an abyss of darkness from which the light of holy knowledge, God's Word, will rescue the fallen and the outcast. Yet Vincent is not, like the prototypic Protestant, one to face God naked and alone: exactly this is what he wishes to avoid. He is slightly manic, he wishes to confront *others* with himself as God's "naked" surrogate. One suspects that, secretly, he is persecuted by the idea (given him in London when his marriage proposal was rejected) that his looks are not personable enough. His face is rawboned, his red whiskers sprout like spikes, and he cannot quiet a certain wild look in his eyes. Having an artist's all-encompassing ego, he cannot forgive himself this lack of personal ingratiation.

Vincent van Gogh, who was ripe to be saved, chose with a kind of transcendent egotism—basically, as I say, the artist's egotism—to project his own crisis on others and to conceive himself as the savior. This unconscious displacement of guilt is common to human experience even if, with increasing education in psychology, it is less frequent in the advanced twentieth century than it once was. Sent by his superiors to the Borinage country in Belgium, Vincent finally settled in Wasmes, where he insisted on imitating the poverty of saints and lived and dressed like the destitute miners themselves. As with all things he did, though he was much in earnest, he managed to overdo the imitation. Instead of soothing and "saving" the miners, he somehow disturbed them. His superiors decided he was "overzealous," and again Vincent was burdened with a humiliating failure: he was dismissed.

There was surely a ready-made métier for van Gogh the evangelist: *others* had succeeded where *he* failed. The nineteenth century offered the greatest opportunity for all sorts of individualism, including the personal métier of evangelism. "Successful" evangelists are with us today. The only answer to the puzzle of Vincent's inspired failure is the presence of an unconscious ineptitude flowing from a self-guilt so great that his vision was trained, not where it belonged, on the world of art, but rather on the moral-religious world. Inwardly, he must have felt degraded much lower than any miner. But rather than embarking on a course of self-retrieval, he had imagined, with his frantic drive, that as salvation's instrument he could be loved and that a mutual love, a collective love, would heal and save him. In this, though the conclusion was extremely bitter, he had to admit that, so far, he had been wrong.

Yet there are limits to the individual's self-indictment after a series of self-superintended failures. In any case van Gogh's great practical problem was "to be loved": this would have solved the moral perturbation that flickered in his eyes and dictated those hasty, impulsive gestures toward people that struck the wrong notes. Yes, he was a marked man long before he became an artist. And (according to the rhythm of this account of him) he was yet to become an artist. At this point, he met and was friends with a Dutch painter, van Rappard. Life itself was very black in Vincent's eyes: art and artists seemed its only illumination. Only one more attempt at marriage was made by this man still blind to his artistic destiny. He asked for the hand of a cousin who had shown a desire to help and sympathize with him. Her refusal was anticlimatic and another shock so great that he became alienated from the idea of marriage and family. He had intuited he might become an artist. The blow from his cousin totally separated him from his parents, as he believed he could never vindicate himself in their eyes.

Commentators generally agree that this was a dramatic turning point in Vincent's life. Now he yielded to a real personal test. And it was, as one might have predicted, perverse in character, vain, a futile confrontation with eroticism. Vincent was in The Hague and, as it were, he loaded the dice against himself by choosing to live with a woman as socially and economically degraded as possible, as if (according to her very name, Christien) he might prove the salvation of a Mary Magdalene. Turbulently,

Groot Zundert—where Van Gogh was born

fruitlessly, he lived with Christien for more than a year and a half. She is the model for a pencil lithograph titled *Sorrow* (1882), reproduced elsewhere in this book. Indeed, taking her, a hopeless drunkard, he had drunk the magic draught which is art. He had become art's addict. It was as if, having secretly married the muse of art, he had made sure of the worthlessness of the muse of religion.

It happened as if automatically. The use of his hands, his heart, his brain, and tacitly all his body, was a *religious* use, yes, but the religion was destined to be (it was already) art. To this activity he decided to give his all: that quintessence of the self of which his other self-gifts had been only parodies, and inadequate. His faith in sexual relations had vanished. In sex, he had found only a living emblem of grief, which he shared as if himself under a penance. He felt impersonal again, the lover of the poor, and during this period, still in Holland, he was to emulate Millet, the great painter of common life, peasant life. Yet it is striking that he was not to evoke from that artist's figures, some of which he copied (see plate 55), the same impassive, subtly self-contained, and very earthy grace. No! His figures would lend peasants no shape of romance, no beautiful integrity or idyllic palette; they would be as ungainly, as uncouth as possible. There is more ironic pity than sympathy in Vincent's works such as *The Potato-Eaters*, especially in one example of this twin subject, where the facial expressions are veiled and cheerless in contrast to the "peasant-cheer" apparent in faces of the other example.

At first, in keeping with despair and misery, a struggling state of sin, his palette is dark as with the black of the earth where miners work. Sunlight seems to have to reach a great distance, and when it arrives, seems to tarnish what it colors. Bright colors are only gradually picked out in patches, almost painfully, like untended flowers growing in hard, sooty ground. If he did not feel an impersonal love for his subjects, one might think from some works that he was bent on creating a cult of the ugly: the coarseness of the painting (see plate 8) and its harsh angularity of line, which later he was to handle like a virtuoso, has now something sodden and dreary about it: a kind of acrid honesty, a little stubborn, a little raw. Tender greens and blues would appear in his palette years later, golden yellows like benedictions from on high. During that period, he was groping out of a shadow. It is as if he were starting to learn over again, in color and form, the lessons that life has taught him to his hurt; only, in terms of

Weeping Woman, 1883

Millet *Sower*, 1850

color and form, these autodidactic lessons were to emerge triumphant: they would heal—if not permanently, for the time being.

He wished to face the truth of peasant consciousness, the truth of their clothes, their bodies, their overlaid "souls." During the early eighties, at Nuenen, he kept up this color and style of compassion in painting. Surely, there is no least condescension, but one senses pity, and in the deviousness of the human mechanism, some *self*-pity. The gospel of the sunshine in painting, the evangelism of Impressionism, had not yet been revealed to him. But since painting is a craft as well as a spiritual art, his hand was busy teaching him the gift of catching a human being in terms of outlines, chiaroscuro, anatomic detail. As if instinctively, Vincent started south and could not resist Paris.

For the first time now, he came here as an artist. He cast himself into the very midst of Impressionism, making friends with Gauguin and Pissarro, meeting Toulouse-Lautrec and Degas. Particularly he found himself interested in the rather arrogant Paul Gauguin, a banker who gave up his business to become an artist. Of them all, however, van Gogh found himself the least successful; he had to go to the Impressionist show at the Durand-Ruel Gallery without seeing himself on the walls. He was destined, in any case, to sell almost nothing during his lifetime. He felt a tremendous attraction, at the Impressionist show, to the work of Monticelli, who painted in heavy small deposits as if handling brilliant bits of earth. Here was something in itself "earthy," the very tactile quality of the canvas surface could transmit the expressivity of the humble, but very present, body; give it a new moral authenticity through the physicality of paint.

A sense of painting as a set of formal procedures different from reality, and yet heightening reality, came to him in Paris. The vogue of Japanese painting, now entrenched with the Impressionists, helped to lead to Post-Impressionism. The formal layout of the Japanese works, their pure color, firm silhouettes against light grounds, and a magic quality of illusion, established a cult for painters who were tired of painting "local color" over and over or reproducing so accurately the atmospheric moods of the French countryside. In the studios, around café tables, and in the shop of old Père Tanguy, where Japanese paintings filled the walls (see plate 17), van Gogh participated greedily in the new aesthetic of exoticism. All this was opening the way for *visionary* pictures. It was what took Gauguin to Martinique and then to Tahiti. Hidden in the various individual styles of

The Sower (after Millet) →

Post-Impressionism was a sort of hedonism, a planned paganism, that occasioned the nineteenth-century revolt against bourgeois convention and localism that would lead to Cubism and Negroism in the twentieth century. In the Neo-Classic drawing of Picasso (post-Cubistic) one may find the beautiful hieratic anatomy of the naked natives in Gauguin's symbolic paintings of Noa-Noa land.

Vincent was to follow his own line, his own destiny. What he acquired in Paris was self-confidence and self-consciousness as an artist with horizons opening into new subjects and new styles. In 1886, the beginning of his Paris period, he copied the spiky handsome portrait of a tree (with flowering trees behind it) by Hiroshige. This moment gave his own style a permanent imprint: see plate 44. While he tended to use casual small flecks of color, and to emulate dot-impressionism in painting the patterns of clothes as well as of burgeoning nature, he was also developing a basic, nervous "armature" of line, distinct as the angular black drawing of the Japanese, but wayward, coarser, much like the Expressionsim he himself would help to create. (See plate 21.) Van Gogh was a pioneer in that consciousness of the isolated stroke — dab, curvet, straight bar — that was to issue in abstract painting of the twentieth century.

As thrilled as was the whole man, van Gogh, by painting in Paris, his private problems—that disturbed seething on the surface of human relations—stayed with him. The nude female model was then part of an artist's life in Paris; such models were usually women "of easy virtue," as the phrase then ran. Surely we find one of these, and significantly an unattractive one, in a naked woman wearing only stockings and shoes, painted by Vincent in 1887. Her body is very commonplace. In a pencil sketch of the same subject, her face is needlessly emphasized by Vincent as repulsive; instinctively one feels that she has been made uglier than she is. In any case, in the oil painting, her wide, crude features are not italicized but blurred, as if all that mattered was, with heavy irony, her body. As an index to Vincent's current attitude toward love, these two works provide a cynical document meaning he had sacrificed all idealism about interpersonal love. The thought is further enforced by what seems the only really pleasing view of the female nude van Gogh ever painted; this was a statue (see plate 14) also done in the Paris period.

Nowadays we live in an era when criticism looks askance at too much "interpretation" of art, or too psychological a slant on latent or explicit

L'Arlésienne, 1890

symbolism. Van Gogh might be thought, by some, devoid of erotic symbolism, anything devious of that sort. Yet this would be a mistake according to the artist's own symbolic interpretations of his work. It was van Gogh, in line with a similar allusion by Gauguin, who spoke of using the paintbrush with the pleasure with which a violinist uses his bow on the strings: it gave him a great "release" of harmonious energy. More than that, as he wrote his brother, Theo, he wished to "express the love of two lovers by a marriage between two complementary colors, their mixture, their oppositions, the mysterious vibrations of close tints." Plate 56 is a confirmation of this.

Again, the work to be called *The Night Café*, done in the Arles period (1888), shows the interior of a small café from whose proprietor Vincent rented lodgings where he spent some of his best and worst hours: where he rested, where he bled. The picture once paid his rent. It is brilliantly lamplit, showing a billiard table dominant and central, its shadow dramatically surrounding it on the floor; the proprietor himself stands by it and a few people are seated inconspicuously at tables against the walls. But what did Vincent (as pointed out by Meyer Schapiro in his highly sensitive study of van Gogh) say of this painting? "I tried," he said, "to express with red and green the terrible human passions." If we did not have the artist's evidence, to how many viewers would it confidently occur that van Gogh meant to indicate passion or vice with the dusky red of the café walls, the greens covering the billiard table, table tops, and other spaces? True, three men seem slumped over, in drunken stupor, perhaps. But the couple at the rear, upright in their seats, display no more "terrible" a human passion than that of having a late drink together. This couple is like many appearing in Vincent's paintings of later years: one is a man, one a woman, and they are isolated together. As for billiards, this game has no reputation for inspiring a passion for gambling; besides, nobody is playing it at the moment.

However obliquely, we must seek in this visionary painter not a symbolism of anecdote or objects with literary associations, but a symbolism of forms, colors, and certain elements of composition. The "lovers' situation" discussed in the comment on plate 56 is virtually unique. Meanwhile Vincent, a painter who "didn't sell," had to depend on his brother Theo for support; his letters to him put his best foot forward and stressed his sincerity, his desire to accept painting as his final choice of vocation.

Moreover, dynamic though Paris was with its painters and intellectual atmosphere, van Gogh's poor health urged him to become a sun worshipper. Soon he tended to see color as a sun in itself. Japanese paintings seemed to proclaim this because they almost totally lacked shadow. The sun, on a bright day in the open and with the air clear, saturated everything — even shadow itself. The newer Impressionists in Paris had begun to understand this and exploit it.

He had despaired of true friendship with women, and love was something that happened to others, to the couples of his paintings. He cherished a dream, however, as he went southward to Provence. There embracing spring, putting its flowering trees on canvas, he thought of having a community of artists with him. He would not live *alone.* Alone, he tended to have temptations of a disturbing kind, strange hallucinations when his mind seemed to unmoor itself from his personality and become some "terrible passion" of its own: a nasty passion, an anti-social passion. Paul Gauguin, at least, must come to what Vincent thought of as a "Studio of the South." And he wanted others, who said they would come but never did.

He had reached Arles and settled there in a house. Here he did the famed two paintings of his bedroom (see plate 46) which symbolize the happiest, most peaceful span of his adult life. The success of his visions, his ability to portray the universal quality he sought in the commonest sights of nature, began now to create a manic stirring in him. It was the frustrated evangelist peeping out again. Instead of a Bible, he held a paintbrush in his hand. That "overzealousness" of which he had been accused, that sign of failure and bitter regret, was translatable in Provence into natural forms that vibrated into waves, that thrust out rays like the sun's — so distinct it seemed one might touch them, break them off. This rhetoric of the brush that gave nature's self new energy — that even could shoot in zigzags like lightning — had nobody to "convert," nobody to save or console. It was simply a paean of praise to glory in nature, not a preachment to natural misery and sin. By the new light in his canvases, human beings themselves were reevaluated: the portraits came. These were not commissioned. He asked people in the town to sit to him. The results are works of love, Vincent's true evangelism, where what is humanly awkward, plain rather than handsome, self-conscious, shy but authentic, with a beauty of sheer being, is enshrined in almost hieratic settings; indeed,

101

some of the backgrounds behind heads are stroked-in sumptuously, glitteringly, as if they were mosaic skies behind Byzantine saints (a deliberate analogy on the painter's part) or gorgeous tapestry behind a queen: see plate 39.

In certain drawings by van Gogh, one can see that he created a geometric physique which the oil painting did not sacrifice but absorbed: the dot or stipple; the straight stroke in rows; the curve; the zigzag. This plastic language is alive on the surface of canvas like the visible bones, muscles, and veins of the human body, so that any one painting is a kind of italicized flesh, a "creature" in action, as if trees and roads, mountains and clouds, were organisms like men and animals. Meanwhile, with all the furious productivity of the Arles period, he had not forgotten the old appeal of peasant dignity, that veiled pathos in which the humblest human life once appeared to him. He copied Millet's *Sower* and *Reaper* and did his own variation on the latter. Life is a drama of creation and destruction. The rich act of reaping, which leads to life-giving bread, also involves death. It is like the cycle of the seasons . . . But here, here in Arles, there is almost no harsh winter.

Yet there is, in Arles, a certain winter of discontent. Gauguin joined him as he desired; they painted and chummed together, even lived together. Quarrels broke out between them. Why? The only true answer is in that outraged disappointment (a hypersensitive powder keg of the spirit) which Vincent could feel when his enthusiasm, his ideas, were snubbed, contradicted, hurled back on themselves. Waves of alarming visions started coming over him. One time he could not prevent himself from throwing a glass in Gauguin's face. The next day he somehow found himself with a razor in his hand, tracking his friend through Arles. Gauguin heard footsteps behind him, turned, and simply stared Vincent down. Half blind with shame and regret, a kind of flame licking his brain, Vincent ran home and cut off his ear with the razor.

He then presented the ear, carefully wrapped, to a woman he proceeded to visit in a brothel. Not only wheat can be reaped! Death, in the old metaphor, is also a reaper, and the result is not the bread of life but the blood of death. Some "terrible passion" of frustration caused his impulse to attack Gauguin and caused its direct result: his attack on himself. He was guilty of the passion that is unspeakable. And his guilt was never, never to leave him. How strange! His painting goes on—his brushes hardly

The courtyard of the hospital at Saint-Rémy

seem to know what he has done, what his thoughts can be. That in itself is alarming: he is more than one person.

One thinks of the many twin figures he painted (see plates 52, 59, and 74): always women, never male couples. At any rate, he felt he had to submit to internment. There was a period at Arles, and then, late in 1889, one in the asylum at Saint-Rémy. Medically, his case was first diagnosed as schizophrenia; later, there were indications that his seizures were a type of epilepsy. So one might infer from some of his most convulsive and flamboyant canvases — as if a "musical" sort of earthquake were taking place. Cypresses seem on fire: stars, moon, and sun behave like comets dashing through the heavens.

Paradoxically, as if dangerous blazes from the sun might ignite him again, he went northward when released from Saint-Rémy and obediently, in Auvers near Paris, allowed himself, at his brother's suggestion, to be treated by a Dr. Gachet. Would one really know from even the most restless-looking canvases that their creator was subject to fits of insanity— to wild destructive impulses? Only if, with ancillary knowledge of his life and death, we study them with their symbolic markings in mind. Of *The Ravine* (plate 59) Vincent himself declared that he conceived the central distant mountain, past the ravine, a looming obstacle: a final bar to passage. A more emphasized mountain exists in plate 60, one almost threatening and oddly like the silhouette of the Church at Auvers (plate 72). Religion! Had "religion" fatally interned him?

He felt, whatever furious drives toward the world his paintings could show, that the world waited to deny him. Conclusive evidence of this is his copy of the Doré engraving called *The Prison Courtyard*, done at Saint-Rémy and depicting prisoners exercising in a circle. The closest prisoner in the moving ring is the only one looking out at us; obviously, though he is beardless, it is van Gogh looking at us. His face has the angle of a three-quarters self-portrait . . . The quivering trees, the pulsing flowers, the sunflowers like semi-extinct suns: the houses and churches as animate as people! These continued for a while on his canvases. But his life was soon over. The three-forked road in his last painting of all (plate 75), done exactly in the tones of *red* and *green* he said represented "terrible human passions," are clawlike fingers reaching for the wheatfield as for the bread of life . . . but being frustrated, frustrated for all time, by the lowering blue sky giving birth to the wings of death.

The house where Van Gogh died (now a restaurant)

Description of the
color plates

1. *Self-Portrait before His Easel*
1888
Oil
65.5 x 50.5cm
Stedelijk Museum, Amsterdam

On what are the painter's eyes fixed? On his subject of course: whatever he is painting. Direct preoccupation with his art has lent a new calm and composure to his features, to his whole demeanor. How steady seems the hand holding the palette and all the brushes! The gaze is just as steady: ultimately solemn. The color values of coat, flesh, and hair are beautifully under the control of Vincent's new, analytical palette. The cool blue of coat has warm gleams; the warm face, cool green shadows that yield gracefully to the torridness of the red beard. This is not the man baffled by his strange, persecutingly barren relations with people and his own human motives. Note the perfect levelness of brows that could easily contract and the unstrained normalcy of lips that could so easily purse in self-doubt or confusion. Here is nothing but the intent craftsman whose sole salvation lies in painting the world.

2. *The Mender*
1881
Pencil and Water Color
62.5 x 47.5cm
Rijksmuseum Kröller-Müller, Otterlo

Here already the dedicated artist is preoccupied with the problem of drawing. The derangement of the shirt being mended has those lines of jagged interest that Vincent was to detect and exploit again and again, much more boldly, in landscape. To some degree, age also has accomplished a "derangement" in the old woman's face — look how the gathered wrinkles of her neck repeat the wrinkles of her skirt gathered at her waist. Here is little sense of the artist's total grasp of figure that was to come later. Considering its subject, the work has an odd absence of pathos. Vincent is now more concerned with detail and detailed execution.

3. *Crouching Youth with Sickle*
1881
Pencil and Water Color
47.0 x 61.0cm
Rijksmuseum Kröller-Müller, Otterlo

Though spiritually Vincent had had an upheaval and was still abashed by the world's challenge, he possessed high confidence in himself and a great unmatured vigor. There is something symbolic in this early male figure as well as an already fine control of action-posture. The wrinkles of the youth's clothes are a bit fussy, not so much from uncertainty of draftsmanship as from Vincent's brooding interest in him and his intent occupation. The landscape is only a shallow backdrop for this occupation: a specific kind that will obsess van Gogh the painter. Yet he will think abundantly of harvesting wheat rather than weeding lawn or garden, and there will be ambiguity in his visions of plenty, the haystacks and the sheaves, and about the sickle as token of death. In the delicate lines and tones here, one perceives the Oriental influence that was gradually taking hold with French painters.

Boulevard de Clichy →
On the Paris Fortification (Page 108)

4. *Woods at The Hague with Young Girl in White*
1882
Oil
39.0 x 59.0cm
Rijksmuseum Kröller-Müller, Otterlo

Already van Gogh has no trouble proving he has the brush of landscape painting well in hand. For its simple layout — almost a genre piece — the picture is extraordinarily rich. The artist has found as much variety in the ground mottled with sun, shadow, grass, and small roots as could well be without seeming overdecorative. The atmospheric tone is completely convincing, the thick tree trunks could not grow more naturally from the earth, the girl's white dress has just the note of luminousness to climax the work's harmonic interest. The perspective of the three trees announces van Gogh's diagonal thrust like a leitmotif.

5. *Fisherman by the Sea*
1883
Oil
50.0 x 32.0cm
Rijksmuseum Kröller-Müller, Otterlo

This image of a young fisherman (as fluent as the water behind him) begins to speak of Vincent's Impressionist simplification: something he would make entirely personal and original. The featurelessness of a face so prominent — the figure being the work's whole subject — itself has the stamp of originality. For this is not a mere sketch, roughly spontaneous as it seems, but a finished work.

6. *The Basket Maker*
Dutch Period
Oil
Private Collection, Paris

Enlivening monochromatic brown with yellow and orange (like gloomy sunlight) seems as far as van Gogh could go, at this early point, toward "making pretty" an image of peasant labor. The blocklike shape of the man's shadow, the heaviness of his clogs, the seeming spareness of his limbs, his air of being "shut off" in the act of working, are all unprepossessing traits for a painting that makes no effort to charm. Vincent had not yet been attracted by Millet — and when he would be, he could not be wholly won to that artist's tranquilly graceful image of labor but (in the very act of copying) would cede him his charm grudgingly.

7. *Leaving the Church at Nuenen*
1884
Oil
42.0 x 33.0cm
Stedelijk Museum, Amsterdam

The style of this acridly colored work has an upright monotony in which detail is more interesting than the whole. Almost dead-center, the church is rescued from stodginess by its conic roof and the variation of the bell tower. As only a set of abstract color splotches, the peasants in the foreground merge with the shadows of the hedge. Vincent is leaving others to grope along a path which he had lost: once he was an evangelist. Compare the gloom here with the singing revelation of the Church at Auvers (plate 72).

In the Suburbs of Paris (Page 109)
← *Harvest on the Plain of Crau*

8. *Head of a Peasant with Pipe*
1884
Oil
44.0 x 32.0cm
Rijksmuseum Kröller-Müller, Otterlo

This work was done when the artist felt convinced he was an admirer of human simplicity such as that pictured by Millet. Yet the actually cubistic drawing of the man's ear, the abstract ruggedness of his knotted neckerchief, the crudeness of his facial lines: all proclaim the kind of turmoil which Vincent must already have been meditating as his own, personal expression of the spectacle of nature, including man. Here he was not at all thinking of charm — the painting has no charm — he was thinking of truth: of a true, and respectful, revelation of humanity.

9. *Portrait of a Young Woman*
1885
Oil
152.5 x 127.0cm
Pushkin Museum, Moscow

By this year, van Gogh had his brushstrokes and his human subjects well in hand. The young woman is herself a living challenge to the world: bosomy — a little obviously so, as if it were part of her profession — with a somewhat vulgar arrangement of red ribbon in her hair, and a profile whose irregularity seems to have been made to order for Vincent's angular drawing. The mouth especially, neither refined nor symmetrical, with a single greedy tooth visible, seems the challenge of a naive devourer — arrogant not from will but from nature itself. Vincent has painted the lusty animal hunger of a human being seen in repose.

10. *Bullock Attached to a Cart*
1884
Oil
57.0 x 82.5cm
Rijksmuseum Kröller-Müller, Otterlo

The artist's earlier lack of flamboyant style is perfectly suited to this bullock attached to a cart. For an honest, inoffensive animal, this specimen is remarkably uningratiating, and van Gogh made not the least effort to flatter it with color or skin pattern or power or friendliness of look. The squinting eyes make it seem a tired beast, withdrawn in servitude, utterly yet awkwardly resigned to its fate. Does something of van Gogh's own soul lurk in this image? He had not yet become his own evangelist.

11. *Cottage at the Day's End*
1885
Oil
65.5 x 79.5cm
Stedelijk Museum, Amsterdam

Only five years or so away from his death, van Gogh had not yet found, in this "tonal" painting of cool greens, warm oranges, and shadow, his palette's supreme variety. Not yet very personal, this country cottage and companioning trees still have extreme assurance. The cottage has some of the humble mystery that gathers about remote country homes at twilight — something dense, uncommunicative, like an outpost of civilization in a wilderness. The trees are graceful, but the house they watch over (peasantlike) is not.

12. *The Potato-Eaters*
1885
Oil
81.5 x 114.5cm
Stedelijk Museum, Amsterdam

The most interesting thing about this and the following plate is that van Gogh should really have duplicated the feat of portraying human earthiness at its homeliest: at this stage, he felt nothing was more sacred. Compared with these peasants, those of Cézanne are intellectual, those of Millet beautiful, those of the Le Nain brothers aristocratic. In this version, the niggardly lamplight highlights the protrusive facets of each face as if the painter detected his serviceability in bringing out the collective humanity as vividly as possible. The work, like its twin, is drenched in the dark of the peasant mind, out of which appears, as it were, the lucid health of animal appetite.

13. *The Potato-Eaters*
1885
Oil
72.0 x 93.0cm
Rijksmuseum Kröller-Müller, Otterlo

This is the same scene as its companion, brought a trifle closer to us. Moreover, there is a remarkable change in the sitters, who seem in personal identity the same as their counterparts (see plate 12). The facial expressions, and the gestures too, are less eagerly, less conventionally, those of hungry people in the act of eating. With downcast or wandering eyes, they are not watching each other as in the other view; especially does the cup-holding man seem dour, apathetic, where his counterpart shows lively anticipation of his drink. One feels that this version followed the other in time; one feels that Vincent, with a pessimistic afterthought, wished to make his subjects more like the humble food before them.

14. *Torso of a Woman*
1886
Oil
73.0 x 54.0cm
Private Collection, Zurich

A classic sculpture, possibly a bathing Aphrodite, headless, armless, legless, impelled Vincent to essay a nude finely sensuous, although stopping short of sensuality or tenderness — a lack due mostly, one may assume, to its being only a statue. The curving sweep of the two-toned background of light brushstrokes aids the figure's leaning movement, while the female rondures and a kind of fingertip feeling for flesh — not emphatic in his portraits of living people — are remarkably well achieved; the hints of warmth in the plaster (or possibly stone) are poetically suggestive without in the least vulgarly hinting of real flesh.

15. *Self-portrait*
1886
Oil
47.0 x 35.0cm
Private Collection, Paris

Predating the self-portrait of plate 21 by a year, here is obviously a study for the same pose and essentially the same mood. Though its manner is not as crystallized, one senses the same solemn intentness of the artist upon an aspect of himself. Vincent has stylishly (it is his mature style) brushed in a dynamic idea that a year afterward will settle beyond doubt the expression of the mouth and the vital nature of the question in the eyes.

16. *Lady beside a Cradle*
1887
Oil
61.0 x 46.0cm
Stedelijk Museum, Amsterdam

Surely van Gogh has "caught" his sitter cleverly: middle-class, well-to-do, a "lady," just a bit smug; a little self-consciously on the edge of her chair as if aware of having her portrait done. While this is a perfectly sound work, one feels the artist's uneasiness with a subject that would have better suited Degas. The veils of the showy, beribboned cradle are, even for van Gogh, rather brashly sketchy. The woman's clasped hands, like a symbol of security in social position, are more interesting than her aggressively vacant gaze. After all, the portrait tells us a great deal about the subject: which is the purpose of portraits.

17. *Père Tanguy*
1887
Oil
92.0 x 73.0cm
Musée Rodin, Paris

Identical in human attitude with the preceding plate, this view of the famous art dealer (a legendary friend of painters) is frontally reassuring and has all the warm sympathy and intimacy lacking to the woman's portrait. One is confronted by a self-contained, wholly benign personality: the familiar folding of the hands in the lap (often found in van Gogh's sitters, as if they could not sit passively otherwise) here has a fresh, unquestionable propriety. The hands are ready to open and "give" because their owner is humanly good. Backed and flanked by the Japanese art that was having a contemporary vogue in Paris, Père Tanguy looks like an exotic king on his throne: these works are verily symbols of his sovereignty. Certainly the rectangular weave of their physical grounds (silk, thatching, heavy paper) suggest the unit of power that van Gogh was helping to enter painting: Cubism. The flakes of snow, the flowers, evoke the dot-and-dab painting of Post-Impressionism—one even begins to feel that the spiky headdress ornaments of the Japanese male and female visible here influenced the style of Vincent's own paintstrokes.

18. *View of Paris from Vincent's Room in the rue Lepic*
1887
Oil
46.5 x 38.5cm
Stedelijk Museum, Amsterdam

The artful contrasts of separate textures here, the architectural self-containment, the orderly conception of foreground and distance, all define a "primitive looking" work as perfectly sophisticated. Yet it is hard to locate its true inspiration unless as a painterly exercise in textures, chiefly stippling. As a given view from a window, it is necessarily a casual composition whose chief purport may be tour-de-force. The irregularity of the closest building's silhouette, at right, seems to have appealed to the artist's love for controlling the difficult. Does the Cathedral of Notre Dame (what else could it be?) in the distance appear to van Gogh as a bird appears to him in the country: as a "winged thought," the fragile soul of something material?

19. *The Yellow Books*
1887
Oil
73.0 x 93.0cm
Private Collection, Swiss

A loose-jointed work, this gives the present viewer at least the wayward idea that the stipple and its vertical and horizontal extension (characteristic of van Gogh) have something to do with this painter's conception of words and is not (as with all sorts of dot impressionism) a matter of portraying atmospheric modes of light and color. We see, beyond the books, patterns of hanging rugs, themselves woven. Yet what all painters of this period in France took from Japanese painting tended to blend hieroglyphically into rendering of texture and outline. Only the two roses at right, oddly upright, isolate themselves from the pervasive feeling that the books here have lent their lines of print to the surroundings.

20. *Flowers in Blue Vase*
1887
Oil
61.0 x 38.0cm
Rijksmuseum Köller-Müller, Otterlo

This vase of flowers has the assurance and suavity of the most confidently handsome works of the same subject by Impressionists. Its equilibrium of color and form, its communicative lushness, are just as triumphant. Oddly, some flowers here are a trifle insubstantial (as are Redon's), as if suspended in air rather than attached to a stem supported by a vase. But the painting has van Gogh's plastic signature. One notes how he has utilized the peculiar character of each kind of petal to suggest his stipple as well as his long stroke. The all-yellow daisies are like his suns, those with downward-drooping petals like his tree branches (see plate 43) inverted.

21. *Self-portrait (detail)*
1887
Oil
32.0 x 23.0cm
Rijksmuseum Kröller-Müller, Otterlo

Somewhat like a movie close-up, this detail, concentrating on the artist's own face, emphasizes the ominous anxiety that spreads from the half-contracted brows to the barely compressed lips. The whole image, humanly considered, is like a warning, and as a self-portrait amounts to alerted self-solicitude. "Who *am* I?" it seems to say in the soberest of tones. And: "What lies just ahead?" In the way the paintstrokes fan out from the mouth to beard and lapels . . . reconcentrate as the tie begins, are newly accented by the collar's diversion and congregate more subtly on the face as lines of character merged with highlights . . . we have an impressive example of a twin efficiency: form and ruthless self-inspection.

115

22. *The Bridge at Chatou*
1887
Oil
52.0 x 65.0cm
Private Collection, Zurich

Were it not for the peculiar lean-to of various architectural elements of this land/water scape, it would have a layout typical of the high Impressionists. Yet van Gogh's analytical palette was never quite as even as that of Monet, Pissarro, Renoir, or others. Nobody but Vincent would have made the coquettish figure of the pink lady with red parasol (is the train's engineer on the bridge sending her a flirt's message?) so tightly monochromatic a contrast with the work's prevailing blue and ochre; also, the idiosyncratic length of the artist's single stroke (waywardly directed as usual) peeps out from — and salts — a picture that otherwise would look like a genre piece shared with many others.

23. *Lark over Wheatfield*
1887
Oil
54.5 x 65.5cm
Stedelijk Museum, Amsterdam

At first sight, something that might be a detail announces itself as an expression of van Gogh's musicianly command of the stroke (which is also a kind of caress) to interpret a symphonic aspect of a bit of nature that would escape the attention of other artists. At this moment, his art is in full stride. The hovering bird, so masterfully characterized, is like a thought in its first intuitive form. This rather green wheat vibrates with a breeze that modulates it only with exchanged promises. Even the withered foreground of vestigial stalks has a way of renewing lost vibrations to mingle with the song of energy being absorbed by the sky, which itself is seeded with cloudlets.

24. *Caravans at a Gypsy Camp*
1888
Oil
45.0 x 51.0cm
The Louvre, Paris

Here we have a study more than a reassuringly complete conception: a piece of spontaneous observation of communal life that seems to hold for the roughly susceptible Vincent some attractive secret from which he was excluded. The shadows here conspire to keep the gypsies, with their legend of determined estrangement, safe from the painter's eyes and from the eyes of all. This exclusiveness is accentuated by the startling bareness of the foreground with its seemingly useless geometric outline of what might be the ground-plot of a "permanent home."

25. *Truck-gardens*
1888
Oil   73.0 x 92.0cm
Stedelijk Museum, Amsterdam

During the year at Arles, Vincent attained his most brilliant sunlight-palette. What begins by seeming a few things, ends by being more than a few: this distinguishes a masterfully equilibrated landscape from looking like a beautifully typical work of the

Impressionist school. These things are the assertive linear accents that anticipated, by so many decades, the abstract-expressionist style: the spiky trees; the discontinuous wavy sides of roofs and buildings; and above all, the expressionistic daring of the ladder against the haystack at left and the drawing of the cart wheel at center (a relative of the more savage cart wheel of plate 64). Even the drawing of the distant horse (with cart) is indelibly Vincentian. Yet finally we are left with the lyric placidness of our first impression in which details are sacrificed to the whole. The painting is as consummate in balanced composition as an irreproachable sonata. Vincent thought of the violin when painting.

26. *Orchard in Bloom, Bordered by Cypresses*
1888
Oil
65.0 x 81.0cm
Rijksmuseum Kröller-Müller, Otterlo

Painted in Vincent's less aroused manner, this is almost a decorous Impressionist work, and were it not for the characteristic abstract spikiness of the plants (or are they palings?) in the foreground, one might momentarily mistake its author. Then of course we duly recognize the nervous, oddly irregular flecking by which van Gogh denoted blossoms and how fragile these seem against the sentinel density of the cypresses. Cypresses are cemetery trees, and while they are relatively calm here, the artist could make them as gesticulative as human beings. The phantomlike ladder lying on the ground and the younger tree at left, silhouetting its trunk against the fencing, are grace notes.

27. *Trees in Bloom, Souvenir of Mauve*
1888
Oil
73.0 x 59.5cm
Rijksmuseum Kröller-Müller, Otterlo

A painting of a flowering tree! Pinks against blue sky. One of the most conventional subjects inherited from an immediate past. What has the artist done besides give it his own plastic signature? He has made the angle of vision itself Vincentian. Mathematically the two nearer trees seem too far apart for their lower branches to interlace; yet such is the illusion. So, with a curious oneness, do their blossoms seem to mingle. There might be only *one* tree: the strokes on the ground, vortex-like, lead the eye surely to the nearer of the two. Palpably there *are* two trees. Maybe we are looking at an unintended symbol of the artist's split personality.

28/29. *Bridge at Arles, Pont de Langlois*
1888
Oil
54.0 x 65.0cm
Rijksmuseum Kröller-Müller, Otterlo

Van Gogh may never have met elsewhere with a mechanical structure (the bridge) that so accurately could illustrate the complex dynamic of his brushwork. The picture is a peerless triumph of color and style. The embankment shown is a solid curve-topped mound, abruptly interrupted to permit the passage of the river and surmounted by a mechanical contraption of large posts and metal strips. Much of Vincent's structural sensibility lay in the dynamic split of the "fork," its model being the branching tree. While the horizontal framework of posts echoes the curve of the embankment, they will verticalize themselves on the uprights whenever a boat must pass, and the divisions of the bridge will do likewise. We see a horse-drawn cart with driver exactly at the point where the bridge divides itself. If the bridge opened at this moment, the shock might well separate the horse from the shafts of the cart, and horse and cart might split and fall on opposite sides. At the same time, the organism of the horse-drawn cart, governed by the driver, incarnates all that firm knitting together of energies for which man's ingenuity is responsible. This aspect of the painting is highly sophisticated when compared with the primitive scene in the foreground, where the washerwomen, at a simple manual task, merely disturb with eddies of water the bland face that nature first presented to man.

30. *Yellow House: Vincent's House at Arles*
1888
Oil
72.0 x 92.0cm
Stedelijk Museum, Amsterdam

With a certain studied modesty, a lack of obvious "organization," the artist paints his abode (the corner house) and delicately accentuates the yellow saturation, not only by the intense blue sky but by the dark inside the house. It seems a little irrelevant to make this deep "inside" darkness significant in what is, on the surface, so ingenuous a picture. But the artist's own absorbed admiration for sunlight did not taboo his corresponding (even dangerous) interest in nocturnal dark.

31. *Café Terrace, Evening*
1888
Oil
81.0 x 65.5cm
Rijksmuseum Kröller-Müller, Otterlo

This work, so often seen reproduced, is famous for its intimate bohemianism and dramatic perspective. The illuminated little terrace is an especially reassuring haven for café sitters: the patrons cozily coagulate in contrast with the saunterers in the street; the interest literally plunges (owing to the perspectival emphasis) toward the distant waiter, whose white apron climaxes the staggered ovals of the white table tops. Yet the night beyond, with its exaggerated stars, also has its charm and so do the open shutters above the awning, which seem to receive the starlight with as much welcome as the people under the awning receive the lamplight. Fancifully (it is a picture to breed fancy) the decorous cobblestones are somewhat like tracemarks of feet that have hurried toward the café's glow. To glance at the sky again is like looking forward to today's pure abstraction.

32. *Haystacks in Provence*
1888
Oil
73.0 x 92.5cm
Rijksmuseum Kröller-Müller, Otterlo

With his palette beautifully, surely articulate, van Gogh yielded here to his phalloid preoccupation with stacked hay. One end of a small log, showing on both sides of a pile of boxes at left foreground, is unquestionably a phallic image; the great stacks themselves have the regal shape of coronas. It is a perfectly poised work and can be justly appreciated aesthetically without recourse to any symbolic interpretation. It is simply that a painter is not just a painting machine. He is also a man.

33. *Starry Night on the Rhône*
1888
Oil
72.5 x 92.0cm
Private Collection, Paris

Van Gogh's fascination with celestial bodies as tangible things even to their rays seems most naturally justified in the case of stars, and here, with personal boldness, he has made them and their rays as conspicuous as the lighted houses that cast their own rays through the darkness as reflections on water. There is something mechanically dispersed about this work — and, at bottom right, the strolling couple (appearing like a dim afterthought) do little to give the picture more than it already has: Vincent's tranced admiration for stars shining like flares.

34. *Portrait of a Man*
1889-90
Oil
65.0 x 54.5cm
Rijksmuseum Kröller-Müller, Otterlo

This seems, like a few other portraits of men by the artist, to represent a subject rather shy or dubious about "sitting," one having an ambivalent relation to the man painting him. Or is it just peasant self-consciousness toward so unique an event? One ponders why van Gogh wished to portray so unattractive a person and in the same thought may decide it was because the subject had an attractive brutishness. Vincent had long developed the habit of viewing the homely, even the ugly, as having high pathetic rights of its own. Exactly the artist's response to mere animal life helped him mature that *brusque* quality of line that inseminated a later, official style of Cubism. This portrait may well have been admired by Soutine the Expressionist.

35. *Young Man with a Cap*
1888
Oil
47.5 x 39.0cm
Private Collection, Zurich

Technically one of the artist's best portraits — it has a marvelous integrity — this does not insinuate any of the lurking psychological and emotional agitation that other portraits may betray. Vincent liked the subject, evidently, and thought him a perfect type by which to express the plastic idiosyncrasies of his style: its nervous angularity, its tenderness for irregular emphasis of feature — the nostrils' coarse insistence, the distance between the eyes, the clamped sensuality of the mouth. Throat, collar, and tie (and mouth too) have a remarkably cubistic feeling; indeed, seem to be something Picasso was to admire and acquire.

36/37. *The Sower*
1888
Oil
64.0 x 80.0cm
Rijksmuseum Kröller-Müller, Otterlo

Here Vincent seems to have abandoned any special formal problems for the sake of his seemingly sentimental interest in Millet's *Sower* (of which he did a copy reproduced elsewhere in this book). The present sower, though in the same attitude as Millet's figure, is a boy, not a man, and behind him is a vivid dawning sun. The artist has entirely succeeded in his two limited problems: imparting rough boyishness to the figure and to visible nature a golden-pink saturation of the day's first naked sunlight.

38. *View of Arles with Flowering Trees*
1888
Oil
54.0 x 65.5cm
Stedelijk Museum, Amsterdam

With two trees gesticulative even for van Gogh's trees, this beautifully colored, flatly impressionistic, decoratively detailed picture is one of the artist's minor tours-de-force influenced by the Japanese. The smoothness of the green foreground, dotted with flowers, is coy in comparison with the exuberant angularity of the trees rising from it. So harmonious is the whole, however, that it may take repeated looking to realize that the nearer tree, to the right, seems almost dead, many dead branches apparently having been lopped from it, while the other tree seems young, bristling joyously with branches and blooms. Once more a grim accent has been smuggled by Vincent into an otherwise lyrical picture. Yet note how interesting he has made the hopeless tree by interpreting the death that drenches it with varied color-tones and shadow-patterns.

39. *La Berceuse*
1889
Oil
92.0 x 73.0cm
Rijksmuseum Kröller-Müller, Otterlo

Were the subjects of van Gogh's portraits always shy of him for one reason or another? Or was *he* shy of *them*? This singer of cradle songs, a countrywoman, seems complacently idle rather than watchfully absorbed or meditative, so that her quiescence and her folded hands are ambiguous. Is there not a "vegetable" sort of passivity about her? Maybe the artist has lost, through the years, the quality he originally sought. With bulbous sleeves, bulbous breasts, and a broad shapeless mass of skirt, this woman's suggestion of maternity is ambiguously sentimental. Her oddly shadowed face approaches in texture the tapestry-like look of the florid wallpaper behind her — wallpaper whose pattern is remarkably like the flamboyant night skies Vincent could paint. This artist had his secret and unsecret perversities. Why should so simple a subject seem (it does to at least one viewer) to possess an uncomfortable enigma?

40. *Gauguin's Armchair*
1888
Oil
91.0 x 73.0cm
Stedelijk Museum, Amsterdam

Vincent had rugged and abraded affections for people which at times he expressed by a fetichism for objects associated with them, objects which they touched and owned. Only a few minutes' study of this armchair of Gauguin should be enough to convey that the expressionistic curvatures by which the artist has italicized its original curves tend to make the chair arms embrace and enclose the absent person of Gauguin. Attained partly by precipitate foreshortening, it is as if one's gaze were in the lap of the chair, fastening itself to the upright, lighted candlestick. The foreshortening makes the rung close to the floor in front sag, as if to show that the chair bore a kind of psychic weight that is an echo of the real body sometimes occupying it. The chair itself is as anatomically various as a naked human being.

41. *Sunflowers*
1888
Oil
76.0 x 59.0cm
Private Collection

In sunflowers, Vincent found the same exultant, subtly disturbing thing he so honestly revealed when painting the sun: a central whorl, with branching, veering shafts (the petals). This flower is known for turning its face perpetually toward the sun. Yet, among ten blossoms here, and a bud, there is not one flower that one may confidently say is facing exactly the same direction as another. The centers themselves are in various conditions, both of form and color, and some seem petalless — all bunched effulgence. The light-blue background, really sky-colored, adds to the idea of these sunflowers as various moods of "hours" of the sun itself. The whimsicality of the petals' shapes and directions is voluptuous: almost, in seeming to be spent, cut away from the sun, a voluptuous show of despair.

42. *Park with People: The Poet's Garden*
1888
Oil
73.0 x 92.0cm
Rijksmuseum Kröller-Müller, Otterlo

One might trace in this picture the natural architecture and natural mood that defined the Barbizon School, with its prime absorption in revealing the harmony of an organic world based on leaves and wood. Yet, in analyzing the color, accenting the structure and presenting human figures in a certain everyday subordination to natural surroundings, this work has the sensibility of Impressionism turning into Post-Impressionism. As always, the cumulative diagonal growth of branch from trunk, twigs from branch, and leaves from twigs, has been the artist's chief preoccupation, both doting and detached as that preoccupation was. Leafiness and even the sound of leafiness seems to account for the work's main impact. A thick sibilance seems in the air, not so much the swish of stirred branches as the patient, ceaseless sound of "growing." In the same way, human voices seem to contribute to a wonderful but unheard polyphony.

43. *Pollard Willows* (detail)
1888
Oil
31.5 x 34.5cm
Rijksmuseum Kröller-Müller, Otterlo

Perhaps Vincent's dynamic dance of variantly directed brushstrokes never appeared in simpler choreographic splendor than in such a framed-off detail as this. The daring yet subtle use of primary colors adds to a virile conception of harmonious thrusts in which each discernible unit of a figure seems to be one extended, even if jagged, stroke. This sort of painting is not at all "pretty"; it is only, in being marvelously strong, beautiful. The balance of the palette is as elemental as the balance of drawing with the brush. One does not wonder if the red branches of the distant row of trees indicate blossoms or the sunlit intensity of wood. The water is secure in the shadowy blue intensity of the nearer trees and the brazen sun secure in the yellow of grasses in the foreground. The red is secure in the blood-heat that also drenches this picture within a picture.

44. *The Sower*
1888
Oil
33.0 x 40.5cm
Stedelijk Museum, Amsterdam

This is one of the works whose bold decorative contrasts suggest at once Gauguin's style and Japanese painting. Yet it is far from being either. The modern function of the brushstroke, pioneered by van Gogh, has the faculty (very striking in this case) of shortening the psychological distance between viewer and object at the expense of the illusive distance at which the flat surface of painting aims. Here the image of the world is intimately harsh and dense — the sun not the aerial, buoyant source of light we conventionally think it, but more a colored, textured ball of artificial-seeming flatness. The human figure, a crude and clenched silhouette, is nourishing the ground with seed. Yet in him, and even more, in the curiously defined tree, so Japanese yet un-Japanese with its protuberant twigs and heavy blossoms, nature is shown capable of dark contrariness, unruly thrusts, unexpected challenges.

45. *Self-portrait*
1888
Oil
Private Collection, Zurich

Little of the querulous and ominous elements of other self-portraits of 1888 and 1889 are in this example. Vincent, beardless, looks younger and healthier than seen by himself in the other works. Noticeable here is a subtle but definite physiognomic resemblance to the late modern American painter Jackson Pollock, who in some ways was as turbulent a nature as van Gogh. The mouth here is less "spoiled," the brows more in natural, relaxed position, the stroking itself is easier, less self-assertive than in other self-portraits. The self-inquiry of basic identity ("Who am I?") flows gently, almost serenely, from this face.

46. *Bedroom of Vincent van Gogh at Arles*
1889
Oil
73.0 x 92.0cm
Stedelijk Museum, Amsterdam

One of twins, this justly famous picture — inseparable from the story of van Gogh's life and career — is almost incredibly modest and contains a homely calm quite unlike the legend of his temperament. Maybe the chief element contributing to this domestic sweetness — the most reassuring thing Vincent ever said of himself in paint — is the work's outdoor coloration; the walls are like the sky; the floor, bedstead, and chairs like the sunstruck fields the artist constantly painted. Of course the rectangular nature of furniture gives little opportunity for the peculiar modulation that vexes and glorifies the surfaces of much of this artist's work. Yet the straight sides of table legs and bedboards are accorded the usual nervous pulsation. The room's space is dramatized by exaggerated foreshortening, boldly underlined by the green strokes irregularly denoting the floor planks. The paintings on the wall above the bed (right) define that inward curvature, at once impulsive yet calculated, which seems so much an emotional reflex of Vincent's: an *embrace.* Actually, the dynamic sweep of the foreground reaches a climax in a sort of dislocated vanishing point in the picture on the wall directly above the head of the bed (not the room's vanishing point); the placement of chair/table/chair leads the eye there and so do the hanging clothes jutting up behind the bed. The room is dominated by the bed (the rondure of the red blanket seems to say it is "comfy"), which symbolizes rest with as deep a richness as the violence of van Gogh's genius would allow.

47. *Still Life: Iris*
1889
Oil
92.5 x 74.0cm
Stedelijk Museum, Amsterdam

Only another vase with luxuriant blossoms? Yes, but a highly finished masterpiece in the artist's most personal style. Imagine the picture without the irregular spearlike leaves, and half the variety will seem gone. These long leaves are, as it were, symbols of the deep natural thrust Vincent reflected in his long, self-identifying brushstroke. Yet the idiosyncratic curvet he could give to everything has here been employed to serve a brilliant rendition of a flower form. The shapes of the iris begin to dissolve into variations of Vincent's tree foliage and clouds, and yet not for one moment does one think of them as anything but flowers. Observe the dramatic touch of the broken stalks, which, fallen, point diagonally to bottom right. This is the artist's obsession with showing natural growth cut down: seemingly an inconsequent accident, it lends an important dissidence to the work's conventional propriety.

48. *Still Life with Onions*
1889
Oil
50.0 x 64.0cm
Rijksmuseum Kröller-Müller, Otterlo

The title of the visible book, one about health, is perhaps irrelevant to painting, but it has a shy way (Vincent's way) of pinpointing inconspicuously this artist's insistent preoccupation with nature and things and people as *good*. The commonest utensils, spread about here in a rather loose composition, have a way of saying in one voice that they are homely, friendly — above all: innocent. The picture has a restrained luminosity — no van Goghian wildness at all. Vincent loved this kind of peacefulness among men's things, and perhaps he never stated it more discreetly.

49. *The Alps: Mountain Country near Saint-Rémy*
1890
Oil
59.0 x 72.0cm
Rijksmuseum Kröller-Müller, Otterlo

At a glance, this landscape seems as if windswept — a feeling conveyed by the relative sparsity of brushstrokes, the overall simplicity of modeled volume and the general waviness. The trees at lower right are some of the simplest van Gogh ever painted, while the smaller ones, far left, anticipate the flimsy, flat hieroglyphic curtness of Raoul Dufy's drawing. Strangely, what is most solid, least to be agitated by the elements or altered by time, the mountains, have the liveliest appearance of all. It is as if, in a rather "obvious" landscape, Vincent were deftly emphasizing the affinity between the most transient of things (the clouds) and the least transient (the mountains); only the outlines of the mountains define them as rugged and hard.

50. *Peach-trees in Bloom*
1888
Oil
65.5 x 81.5cm
Courtauld Institute of Art, London

Here, in a work painted in a succession of horizontal layers, mostly between light green and light blue, one sees a remarkable feat of sheer lyric elevation. The greeny-blue opalescence that drenches it has a soprano tone that moves straight up like a voice taking high C. This has been possible because the artist has made the space look wide and empty, nothing very individual interrupting the

bottom-to-top color nuance or the uniformity of sky, distant mountain, blooming peach-trees, fence, and roadside grass. Of course, Vincent has rescued the horizontalism from monotony exactly by the subtle diagonal of the roadside grass passing abruptly from the left corner to the right margin. This contradiction of placid levelness seems to support the purely vertical leap by which we feel organic growth: the change from closed to open bud and the final flower. The whole picture quivers — like a drop of dew on a petal.

51. *Hospital Garden at the Convent of St. Paul*
1889
Oil
95.0 x 75.0cm
Rijksmuseum Kröller-Müller, Otterlo

A work in which masterly prismatic color is perfectly matched with interest of design proclaims itself a serene masterpiece to be compared with the best parallel achievements of Impressionists much calmer in temperament than was van Gogh. The capricious directions of the stroking remain docile to the overall feeling of nature's essential, inorganic quiet, and yet the same brushstrokes lend the scene that palpitance of plant life without which human beings would not sense their kinship with landscape. Vincent's characteristic qualities are seen here best in the tension of the contrasting shapes of tree trunks against the smooth greensward beyond, in the whorl of grass suggested at the very bottom of the canvas and the nervous variations of thickness in the black lines of the building intruding at left. Yet architectural balance is flawlessly conveyed and acts admirably upon the gentle dynamic of the path that starts at bottom left and veers to meet the house.

52. *Cypresses with Figures of Two Women*
1889
Oil
92.0 x 73.0cm
Rijksmuseum Kröller-Müller, Otterlo

The cypresses dominate everything here, and at first glance the two women — who might be twins since they are dressed alike — are not noticed. As always, Vincent's plastic curve has an ambivalence: half convulsive thrust, half restful wave. In an oblique way, perhaps, he felt inspired to personify this dualism with the two female figures, joined as they are. Yet, just because of their understatement, they make one wonder if the picture needed them to complete itself. Like plate 51, this is a work of restrained richness keyed up by the presence of the cypresses. The trees' reddish trunks, with patches of blue sky showing among them, help to concentrate in their foliage a mysterious disquiet.

53/54. *Mower in Wheatfield*
1889

Surely here are the tokens of insanity that had their profound home in van Gogh's soul and stole into his style to unsettle it and

Oil
73.5 x 93.0cm
Stedelijk Museum, Amsterdam

draw upon the miracles of his skill to make his paintings into controlled works. The wheat seems not to mind looking like blond curly hair, or falling waves, but this does not bestow repose on the picture. The outlines of the mountains descending toward the fragile-looking tree (too weak, as it were, to provide a good climax) have a nervous indecisiveness. The center of the work's disturbance is of course the wheatfield, whose wealth of energy a single worker is bent on separating from its source. Vincent certainly had come face to face with the naked dialectic of creation and destruction. The day is ending. The reaper is almost a phantom. Perhaps a resonance from the Bible is meant: "As ye sow, so shall ye reap."

55. *Peasant Woman Binding Wheat*
(after Millet)
1889
Oil
44.0 x 33.5cm
Stedelijk Museum, Amsterdam

The tender, compact, ungesticulative life of Millet's figures, the effect they give, in nature's midst, of solemn quietness answering to solemn quietness, must have been exactly what attracted Vincent to them, since he found in himself the growth of exactly opposite responses. While this sheaf-gatherer's figure is obviously a copy, the lines of her arms and her characteristically Vincentian hands have the knobby angularity (as of contrary forces) that deliberately antagonizes Millet's own draftsmanship. Millet's solid (yet somehow soft) peasants embody the soul of work and of human submissiveness. To this artist coming after him, and arrested before him in admiration, justice seemed to require that nature's lurking antithesis to Millet's thesis be brought to light — and Vincent brought it to light more than once.

56. *The Evening Walk*
1889
Oil
49.0 x 45.0cm
Museum and Art Gallery, São Paulo

From this picture, done in the painter's more offhand manner, one gets the tense feeling that the couple, who might be in a "romantic" situation, are really in a state of emotional disturbance. In an exceptional work, van Gogh has interpreted the basic nervous rigor of his strokes with a mood expressed specifically by human figures. The woman turns her face away from the man and makes an upraised gesture with one arm. It could be an animated conversation — only impersonal mental excitement — and have nothing to do with a quarrel. Nevertheless one feels that in a landscape so welcoming and picturesque, the couple are at odds; there is something jarring about the solid-color contrast of their clothes at an hour when the planet's colors are beginning to blend. The man's red hair and beard identify him as probably Vincent himself. While the two are in step, all else about them seems opposed.

Young Girl With Shawl →

It is odd that the sickle moon literally has the sickle's handle (see plate 54). The moon is something for lovers traditionally to implement — but the sickle *cuts down*.

57. *Grove of Olive Trees*
1889
Oil
72.0 x 92.0cm
Rijksmuseum Kröller-Müller, Otterlo

The beautiful tonalities here between blue and green seem a tribute to the natural absorption of air by plant life. Instantly communicated to the viewer, I feel, is an image carrying simply a bountiful excitement in the process of growth. The modulations of the ground dance with the jauntiness of the triumphantly leafing little trees while the leaves, at top, seem (in typical van Gogh manner) to merge like flames with a mutually aroused, and equally rhythmic, sky.

58. Olive-gathering
1889
Oil
73.0 x 92.0cm
Rijksmuseum Kröller-Müller, Otterlo

The heightened green palette shimmers quietly, more prismatically here than in the foregoing plate: the olive trees have borne their fruit and workers pick them. From the silvery blue tints on the ground, like translucent slate, it seems to be late afternoon. Rusty hints in the sky and the yellow green glow on the horizon suggest a moment near sunset. The energy of the trees looks relatively contained. All work, of day and season, is ending. Vincent's twist of brush is as if "hushed" here by the overspreading dim opalescence.

59. *Ravine in the Peyroulets*
1889
Oil
72.0 x 92.0cm
Rijksmuseum Kröller-Müller, Otterlo

The palette of the artist's friend Gauguin seems to share the tapestry-like surface achieved by Vincent's characteristic stroking, which here adds a spotty discontinuity to its distinct thrusts as if they were signs of heavy, interwoven threads. The undulant energy of the wave that defines the artist's style has, rather surprisingly, a special "sculptural" beauty in this work, where the evenly applied brushing would seem to wish, on the contrary, to flatten things. The theme is beautifully marked by the apertures of the rocks (like the mouths of caves) next to the stream. The stream itself flows out of the picture toward us; the mountains and their verdure seem to flow steadily toward the sky and the horizon. As usual, the two human figures (again two women) come as a surprise and remain as a minor enigma. For Vincent they may personify nature's annoying, inescapable duality.

60. *Wheatfield with Tree in the Mountains*

One feels somehow that the artist in his mentally disturbed state was beginning to reflect certain tensions in the world (here man's

1889
Oil
73.0 x 91.5cm
Rijksmuseum Kröller-Müller,

creations versus nature's) that were not before so distinctly crystallized in plastic terms. There is here a curious antagonism between the rather overassertive shape of the blue mountain and the similar, yet firmly different, shape of the house that is directly below it. Gradually, too, one becomes aware of the "deprived" state of the poor tree that has been cut down to a mere forking stump. The graduated palette (mostly succulent greens backed by reddish shadow) serves to disguise the picture's inner tensions.

61. *The Resurrection of Lazarus*
(after Rembrandt)
1889
Oil
48.5 x 63.0cm
Stedelijk Museum, Amsterdam

Rembrandt's preoccupation with sunlight doubtless prompted van Gogh's interest here, but what his great countryman felt in a studied way, Vincent felt spontaneously in his awkward-casual style of drawing. The woman herself is as golden as the sun, and maybe van Gogh (the love-leper) forlornly imagined the entrance of some richly maternal, powerful woman who would revive him from the death-coma of repeated rejection by women. There is abundant life in the golden-haired woman.

62. *The Good Samaritan* (after
Delacroix)
1890
Oil
73.0 x 60.0cm
Rijksmuseum Kröller-Müller, Otterlo

Van Gogh has given us one of the most remarkable copies in all painting: something that might almost have been his. The colors are his own although the expressive physical postures, so accurately portraying actual shifts of held and holding weights, are only his vivid match for Delacroix's rendering. Perhaps here Vincent divined the moral function concentrated in his aborted past career as an evangelist. Nature's nervous, pulsating inequities could be governed, "righted," by a pure strong act of good will in taking over another's burden. But this year his suicide will come — now, far from being a savior, he needs one.

63. *Haystack after a Rainy Day*
1889
Oil
64.0 x 52.5cm
Rijksmuseum Kröller-Müller, Otterlo

A painting, this, daring in the simplicity of its enterprise, which in sum is to present two dominant forms (the yellow haystack and the blue shadow of a large cloud) that echo and contrast with one another. Is this not van Gogh's version of the shadow and the substance? Nor can we miss that this haystack, in shape and texture, is at a distance where it seems the loaf of bread it will synthetically become. It also, in look, is impressively, if passively, phallic. And so was, if we examine the issue, the aspect of loaves made sacred to pagan ceremonies. Surely, nothing about the mature Vincent — now about a year away from suicide — should frighten or astonish us. And above, as if arriving at a signal, are the fatal death-designing crows that will overwhelm the wheatfield which is to be an immediate token of Vincent's suicide.

64. *Road with Cypress and Star* (detail)
1890
Oil
92.0 x 73.0cm
Rijksmuseum Kröller-Müller, Otterlo

This detail displays the intense architectural energy van Gogh gave every inch of his canvases. Not to be mistaken for a young child's work, the contents of this rectangle nevertheless suggest the casual, bold, arbitrary drawing of the child — particularly the shape of the house and the cart's wheel. Haste of execution *seems* rather than *is* here: a sort of offhand demonstration of mastery over the minutiae of form and style. In many ways, the images are not attractive, surely not ingratiating, yet like certain works of children the painting presents the world as a simple set of solid existences — beyond irony, grace, judgment, or even naïveté.

65. *Dr. Gachet's Garden*
1890
Oil
73.0 x 52.0cm
The Louvre, Paris

The painter is at Auvers. It is the year of his death. This wonderfully controlled work might be called an image of liberated tensions. The long-leaved, arabesque plants and the waving cypress are ideal forms for expressing the high rhythmic pulse that plagued Vincent's bloodstream and sought an exteriorization it never truly found in human and social terms. With its boldly diagonal red wall, its welter of abstract strokes, this painting is a casual cadenza by a master artist. The rounded dabs of the red flowers, set against the thrust of the plant leaves, serve as diminishing notes in the work's rich musical phrasing.

66. *Grieving Man*
1890
Oil
81.0 x 65.0cm
Rijksmuseum Kröller-Müller, Otterlo

This work identically echoes the posture in a drawing of a woman seven years earlier, but the present subject may well be a fellow patient at Saint-Rémy. Life itself seems to have paled for the warm and cool palette here, which for the van Gogh of 1890 is faint. The unity of draftsmanship is pronounced — shoes and hands, especially, but also the treatment of the hair and the flames in the grate, which have a curious affinity to one another. Even the shoelaces have the wayward twist of the artist's signature. Notice how the shadows of the clenched hands, some of the strokes in the trousers, and the ignited pieces of wood chime with a difficult sort of rhythm. Human nature and the nature of field and sky shared a kind of resigned, self-contradictory harmony of being which, for Vincent himself, would explode into the desire to end a life that had never attained inward unity.

67. *Field of Poppies* (detail)
1890
Oil
71.0 x 91.0cm
Kunsthalle, Bremen

We have an authoritative detail showing the painterly conscientiousness of the superb craftsman that van Gogh was. No detail of distance or unit of burgeoning nature has been too unimportant not to receive its own treatment. Every bit of organic texture has been worked out in relation to Vincent's final style, where the paintstroke is both independently abstract and interpretive of nature. One spontaneously admires the achievement: here was a master painter who could bring the greatest finesse, the most meticulous precision, to an *apprehension of roughness*.

68. *Study of Cows*
1890
Oil
55.0 x 65.0cm
Musee des Beaux-Arts, Lille

Sheer observation of nature rather than any dominant plastic conception commends this picture to us. The colors are monotonous and not especially appealing. The drawing of the animals is quintessential van Gogh, however, and clairvoyantly cubistic — as, indeed, were the bulls of certain Paleolithic cave paintings. One notes with amusement how perversely human the face of the top cow is: it might be a caricature by Picasso! The relation of the two cows at bottom is delightfully accurate; one nuzzling, the other tossing away her head.

69. *Street in Auvers*
1890
Oil
73.0 x 92.0cm
National Museum, Helsinki

Each modern painter having a vein of expressionism tends to anthropomorphize things, to alter their passive inanimacy to gratuitous "gesturing." Utrillo did it to the faces of buildings in the quietest, most elusive way of all. But here, van Gogh's avoidance of the straight line of architecture saturates a picture, quite without human beings, with a transcendent humanity. We see a world manmade. His control of this process is itself magical: a fact pointed up, with plastic arrogance, by the inverse geometry of angular rather than rounded clouds made by a sky of blue rectangles. Together with the wilfully whimsical trees, this work, I should say, illustrates a grandly modest pyrotechnics blending nascent Cubism with nascent Expressionism.

70. *Landscape with Three Trees and a Cottage*
1890
Oil
64.0 x 78.0cm
Rijksmuseum Kröller-Müller, Otterlo

The cloud shaped like one of Vincent's female torsoes (see *La Berceuse*), the hillocks like waves and ribbons, the tree foliage like flames, this is "formula Vincent," so easy to look at, so easy to have done if you were van Gogh. Are works such as this "minor," tacitly or untacitly to be desiderated? It depends. Truthfully, this particular work has the charm of those beautiful spontaneities — dispensable but invulnerably authentic — without which the repertoire of a master would seem less than full.

71. *Cottages at Cordeville*
1890
Oil
73.0 x 92.0cm
The Louvre, Paris

Perhaps in no other single work of van Gogh do we look so surely on a landscape and yet take in also, to an enchanted satisfaction, that unique calligraphy, that purely linear ebullience, he gave to all things, rounded or rectangular, massive or fragile, more or less isolated, more or less merged. This painting exudes the harmony known as style as a flower exudes its odor. In general, a gamut of light-carrying greens, the blue of its sky, the dusky ochre of its stacked hay, set firmly in place those necessary accents by which the natural spectrum universalizes itself.

72. *The Church at Auvers*
1890
Oil
73.0 x 92.0cm
The Louvre, Paris

An interesting question is: Does the witnessing woman in this picture perceive its drama or is the drama reserved only for a fortunate élite? Van Gogh has a fascinating way of posing this question over and over. Dominating one of his really great works, this piece of sacred architecture seems to refine, with most extraordinary beauty, the element of man's aesthetic contribution to the pre-human condition of the planet. The church is a dream of plastic invention. Structured oddly like the looming hill in plate 60, it seems drenched in its own luminous shadow, with a light coming from beyond the planet, like the neo-Platonic reflection of heavenly things by earthly. The coarseness of the Vincentian long-stippled foreground only helps to unify the church's paradoxical gleam, the light-blooming shade of which it is made as much as by architecture. And the sky, remarkably bland for van Gogh, deep and "unproblematical" as a peasant's religious faith — it is much like the sky of the doom-painting: *Wheatfield with Crows.*

73. *The House at Auvers*
1890
Oil
50.5 x 101.0cm
Stedelijk Museum, Amsterdam

There is a challenging commonness about this landscape. A very minor van Gogh, it is indelibly his. So shallow seems its inherent interest, it might almost be a decoration for a screen. If one thing distinguishes it, it is the hint of precipitate foreshortening in the flat foreground, something much more conspicuous as typical of van Gogh in the following plate. It is as if the ground suddenly "opened" — not literally, in the shape of a cliff or cavern, but in terms of inviting one's entry. Vincent finally stood — avid, frustrated, with little hope — on this open threshold of nature. The emotion will be consummated in his very last painting.

74. Staircase at Auvers
1890
Oil
49.8 x 70.0cm
City Art Museum, St. Louis

Again we have the artist busy converting a natural perspective, with houses and people as well as greenery, into a throbbing melodrama of swiftly converging lines as if all things hastened to some climactic meeting . . . Yet just where, and what, is the climax? We sense clearly here that van Gogh always felt the vanishing point as a kind of vortex which pulls the vision toward it at a speed of undulant excitement. We must ponder over the two groups of women (a pair of girls and a mature pair) whose twin-ness is a tantalizing feature of the artist's repertoire. The most artificially wavy lines here are those of the staircase, where a male pedestrian's feet are illusively close to one woman's hat, which marks the picture's center. In a scene all surface simplicity, something reaches out to grip us with its mystery.

75. Wheatfield with Crows
1890
Oil
51.0 x 103.5cm
Stedelijk Museum, Amsterdam

Every stroke in this work, painted only a little while before the artist shot himself, seems based on the flying form of the bird of death, the crow, which appears here in quantities and contributes to the unusual depth of the dark-blue sky as if it had materialized from it. Now, at the end, Vincent has revealed all perceptible nature in terms of an ultimate reduction to abstraction: the crows are simply "birdlike" arrangements of his zigzag line. The road has three forks; the central one, leading to infinity, is lost amid the crowding, sun-golden wheat; the others disappear to right and left as if into realms of possibility. The "crotch" of the fork seems exactly beneath the viewer's feet — as if he stood there with the artist. Here that curiously greedy precipitance of perspective, found in so many of van Gogh's pictures, becomes stronger, more intimate, than ever. Gorgeously tactile, the natural voice of the picture seems to speak to the soles of the feet and to the soul.

76. Portrait of Dr. Gachet
1890
Oil
66.0 x 57.0cm
The Louvre, Paris

Visible emphatically above the waist — not usual in van Gogh's figure portraits — Dr. Gachet is portrayed as decidedly a "thinker": the perplexed eyebrows, the half-vacant, transparent, speculative gaze, the fisted hand to cheek, the impatiently (or is it cynically?) pursed lips: all these signify the world's conspiracy to come mentally to Vincent's rescue. The doctor's left hand, somewhat greenish in tone like the plant sprig it touches, is the "feeling" hand; the right, blooded wholly with humanity, the "thinking" hand. Vincent knew, through his own experience and intuition, that mankind is thus divided and is indissolubly, disquietingly thus united. It is a spiritual *self*-portrait.

About the author: Parker Tyler has written widely on art for more than twenty years. He has appeared frequently in *The Magazine of Art, The American Artist, Arts Digest,* and *Art News* (of which he was editorial associate, 1954-1958) and was managing editor of *Art News Annual* for two years. He is the author of *The Divine Comedy of Pavel Tchelitchew* (1967), *Florine Stettheimer: A Life in Art,* a monograph on Conrad Marca-Relli, three books of verse, books of film criticism, and a book of literary essays. His poetry is represented in important anthologies, and his essays on the film appear in literary and film anthologies. He received a citation from *The Nation* for his book *Chaplin* (1948) and from *The New Republic* for his play *The Screen.*

Photographed by André Held (plate 17) Photographie Giraudon (6,9,14,15,19,22,24,35,45,56,65,67,68,69,76) Rijksmuseum Kröller-Müller (2,3,4,5,8,10,13,20,21,26,27,28,29,31,32,34,36,37,39,42,43,48,49,51,52,57,58,59,60,62,63,64,66,70) Amsterdam Stedelijk Museum (1,7,11,12,16,18,23,25,30,38,40,44,46,47,53,54,55,61,73,75,78) Toshio Ushiyama (50,71,72,77) Zauho Press (33,41,74)